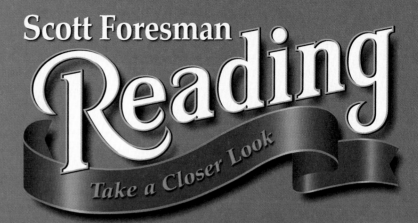

Scott Foresman
Reading
Take a Closer Look

Good Times We Share

Take a Closer Look

Let's Learn Together

Favorite Things Old and New

Take Me There

Surprise Me!

About the Cover Artist
Maryjane Begin and her family live in Providence, Rhode Island, where she teaches college students when she is not working on her own art. Many of her illustrations—even of imaginary places—show how things in Providence look.

ISBN 0-673-62154-5

4 5 6 7 8 9 10-VH-06 05 04 03 02 01 00

Scott Foresman Reading
Take a Closer Look

Program Authors

Peter Afflerbach

James Beers

Camille Blachowicz

Candy Dawson Boyd

Deborah Diffily

Dolores Gaunty-Porter

Violet Harris

Donald Leu

Susan McClanahan

Dianne Monson

Bertha Pérez

Sam Sebesta

Karen Kring Wixson

Scott Foresman

Editorial Offices: Glenview, Illinois • New York, New York
Sales Offices: Reading, Massachusetts • Duluth, Georgia • Glenview, Illinois
Carrollton, Texas • Menlo Park, California

Contents

Take a Closer Look

🎗️ **The Nap** **10**
animal fantasy
by Helen Lester
illustrated by Jackie Urbanovic

🎗️ **Oh, Cats!** **18**
rhyme
by Nola Buck
illustrated by Nadine Bernard Westcott

4

Look at That! 42
realistic fiction
by B. G. Hennessy
illustrated by Seth Larson
Science Connection

Can You Find It? 50
realistic fiction
by Sharon Fear
illustrated by Wendy Edelson
Science Connection

 ## What Did I See? 68
realistic fiction
by Helen Lester
illustrated by Benton Mahan

I Went Walking 76
patterned text
by Sue Williams
illustrated by Julie Vivas

Quack, Quack! 107
poem
by Dr. Seuss

Unit 2

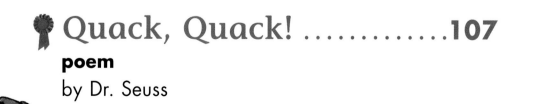

Fish Mix 110

photo essay

by Judy Nayer

Science Connection

🎗 How Many Fish? 118

realistic fiction

by Caron Lee Cohen

illustrated by S. D. Schindler

Science Connection

One, Two, Three, Four, Five 139

classic poem

a Mother Goose rhyme

Jog, Frog, Jog 142

animal fantasy

by Barbara Gregorich

illustrated by Bernard Adnet

Tadpole to Frog 150

expository nonfiction

by Fay Robinson

Science Connection

Notice 159

poem

by David McCord

A Big Job 162

realistic fiction

by Kana Riley

illustrated by Stacey Schuett

Science Connection

Sweet Potato Pie...........170

rhyme

by Anne Rockwell

illustrated by Carolyn Croll

Pictionary: Animals 190

Word List 192

Unit 2

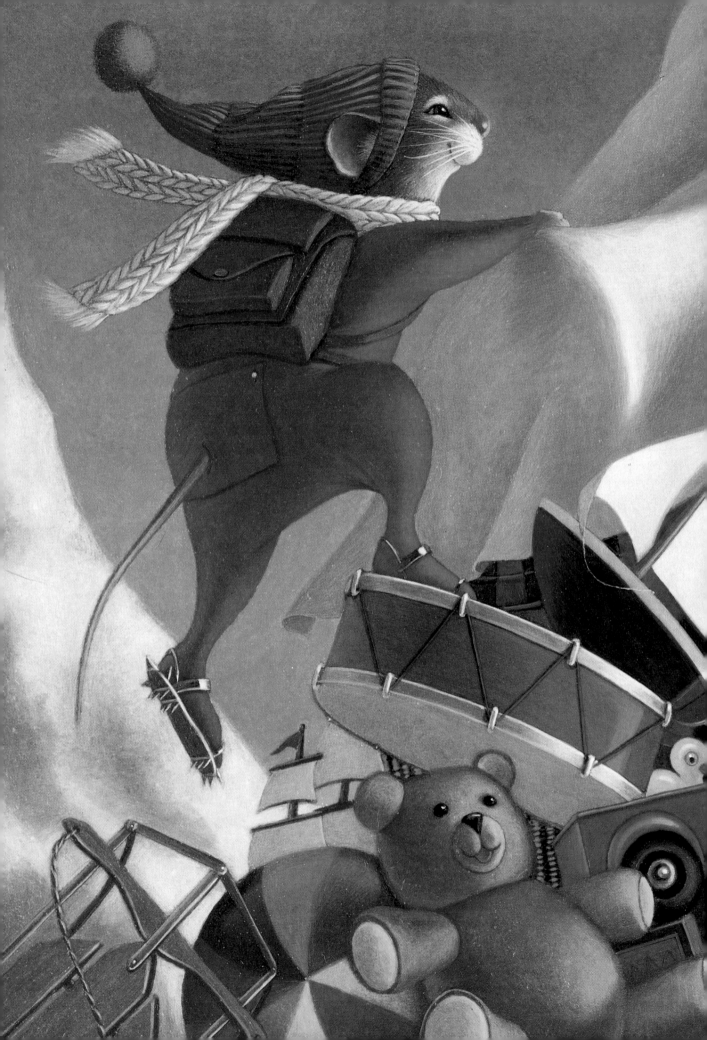

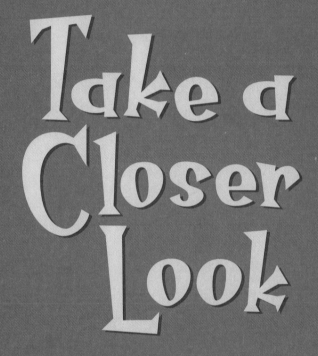

Take a Closer Look

Look closely!
Now what can
we see?

The Nap

by Helen Lester

illustrated by Jackie Urbanovic

I am on my mat.

I will have a nap.

Away I go.

Look at that!
Wag, wag, wag.

I like my cap.
Can I have the bat?

Will it go up?
Will it come down?

No. Not on the dad!

No. Not on the cat!

Look at that!

What a nap!

Oh, Cats!

by Nola Buck

illustrated by Nadine Bernard Westcott

I can see cats.
One, two, three cats.

I can say cats.
Come and play, cats.

Up you go, cats.

No, no, no, cats.

Where are you, cats?
I see two cats.

I will come, cats,
to find one cat.

Now I see cats.
One, two, three cats.

You come down, cats.
Come down now, cats.

Jump and play, cats.

Run away, cats?

No, no, no, cats.

Do not go, cats.

If you stay, cats,
we will play, cats.

Up to you, cats.
Be my new cats.

Like you so, cats.

Oh, cats!

About the Illustrator

Nadine Bernard Westcott liked to draw as a child. She did "sketches on the back of restaurant paper place mats."

When she was a child, she dressed her cat in doll's clothes. How would the cats in the story like that? Now she likes to draw cats.

Let's Talk

How would you make the cats stay?

Name a Cat

Which cat in the story would you like to have? Draw its picture. Give your cat a name.

Patches

Animals at Play

A **sentence** is a group of words that tells a complete idea.

A sentence begins with a capital letter. Many sentences end with a **.** .

The cat ran **.**

This is a sentence.

It tells what the cat did.

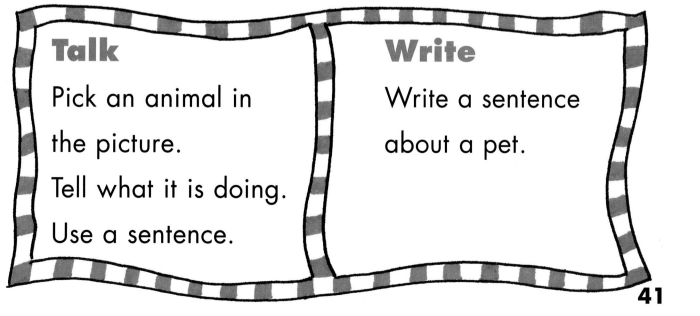

Talk

Pick an animal in the picture.

Tell what it is doing.

Use a sentence.

Write

Write a sentence about a pet.

Look at That!

by B. G. Hennessy
illustrated by Seth Larson

I like to look at clouds.

Do you?

Look at all the clouds.

Look at the clouds play.

Look at that cloud!
Can you find a hat?
I see a hat on a cat.

Look at that cloud!

Can you find a man?

I see a man and a pan.

Look at that cloud!
Can you find a cub?
I see a cub in a tub.

Look at that cloud!
Can you find a bear?
I see a bear in a chair.

Look at all the clouds.

The clouds are big and fat.

Those clouds make rain.

I like to look at rain.

Do you?

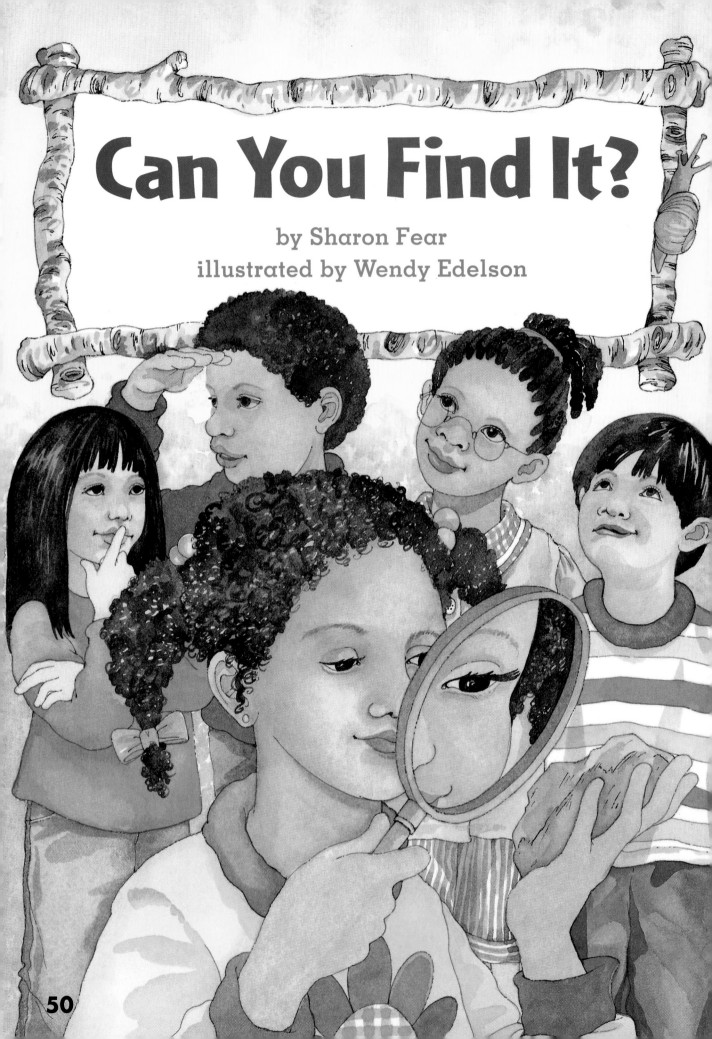

Can You Find It?

by Sharon Fear

illustrated by Wendy Edelson

Make a snack.

Make a map.

Get a hat.

Get a bag.

Come with us.

Play with us.

We are all friends.

Find the snail!

Can Sam find a snail?

Not in a web.

A spider is in the web.

Can Pat find a snail?

Not in a nest.

A bird is in the nest.

Can Jan find a snail?

Not in a hole.

An ant is in the hole.

Can Nat find a snail?

Look at that!

A snail is on the leaf.

Come with us.

Play with us.

We are all friends.

Find the snail!

About the Author

Sharon Fear and her family lived on a farm. Later they moved to a ranch. Her neighbors liked to tell and retell stories. "Maybe that's where I learned to love stories so good that you could tell them again and again," says Ms. Fear.

Start

Reader Response

Let's Talk

The children in the story look for snails.
What animal would you want to look for? Why?

Find the Snail

1. Make a snail from clay or paper.
2. Hide all the snails.
3. Have a snail hunt.
4. Where did you find the most snails?

Look Around You

Every sentence has a naming part.
The **naming part** names a
person, animal, or thing.

The girl looks.
A boy finds ants.

Talk

Look at the picture.
Tell about a person,
animal, or thing.
Use a sentence.

Write

What animal can you
find near your home?
Write a sentence about it.
What naming part will
you use?

67

What Did I See?

by Helen Lester

illustrated by
Benton Mahan

I went to the park.

What did I see?

I saw a slide.

Slip!

I saw a ball.

Kick!

I saw a duck walk.

Quack!

I saw a big hill.

I win!

I saw a tree.

I hid!

I saw a rock. Oh, no.

Trip!

I saw kids.
Lucky me!

I Went Walking

by

Sue Williams

illustrated by

Julie Vivas

I went walking.

What did you see?

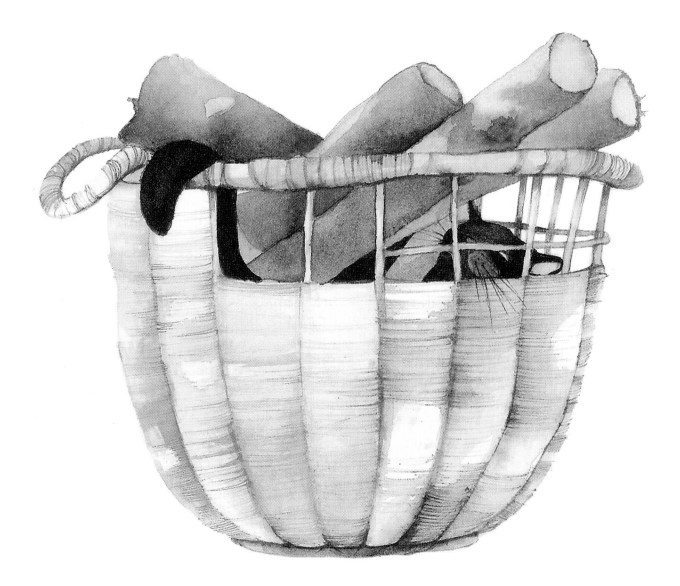

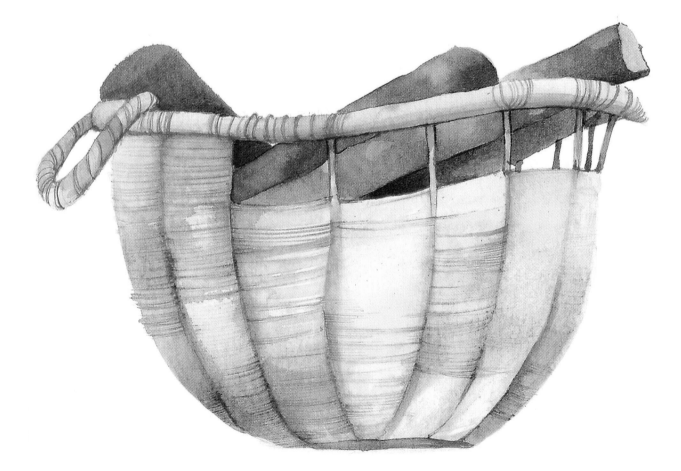

I saw a black cat
looking at me.

I went walking.

What did you see?

I saw a brown horse
looking at me.

I went walking.

What did you see?

I saw a red cow
looking at me.

I went walking.

What did you see?

I saw a green duck
looking at me.

I went walking.

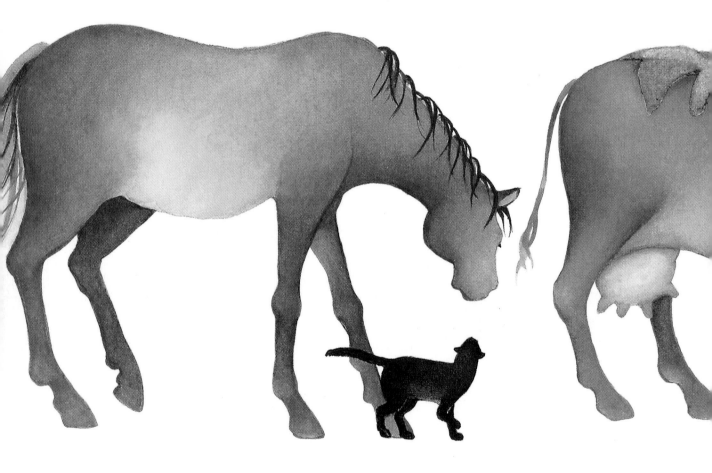

What did you see?

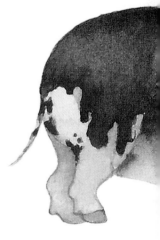

I saw a pink pig
looking at me.

I went walking.

What did you see?

I saw a yellow dog
looking at me.

I went walking.

What did you see?

I saw a lot of animals
following me!

About the Author and the Illustrator

Author

Illustrator

Sue Williams lives on a farm. She raises sheep and grows apples. *I Went Walking* is her first picture book. She wrote it for her nieces and nephews.

Julie Vivas begins her pictures with pencil. She finishes them with watercolor. She says, "I enjoy the wet paint melting into the wet paper."

Quack, Quack!

by Dr. Seuss

We have two ducks. One blue. One black.
And when our blue duck goes "Quack-quack"
our black duck quickly quack-quacks back.
The quacks Blue quacks make her quite a quacker
but Black is a quicker quacker-backer.

Let's Talk

Which animals in the story have you seen?

Animal Colors

Draw an animal you saw as you went walking. What color will you make it?

What We Do

A sentence has two
parts. It has a naming
part and an action part.
The **action part** tells
what the person or
thing does.

A boy **reads**.
A girl **paints**.

went
walk
saw
did

Talk

Look at the picture.
Tell what someone is
doing. Then tell what
you do in school.

Write

Work with your class.
Write about what you do
in school. Use sentences.
What action parts will
you write?

Fish Mix

by Judy Nayer

I see one fish.

I see two.

I see three fish.

Will they swim to you?

How many yellow fish?

How many blue?

I see a mix of fish.

How about you?

Six little fish.

They swim like this.

One big fish.

Its fins go swish!

A mix of fish!

Why do they stop?

I see why!

A man is on top!

How Many Fish?

by Caron Lee Cohen
illustrated by S. D. Schindler

How many fish?

How many fish?

Six little fish in the bay.

Where do they go?
Why do they go?

Six little fish on their way.

How many feet?
How many feet?

Six little feet in the bay.

Where do they go?

Why do they go?

Six little feet on their way.

How many fish?

How many fish?

One yellow fish in the bay.

Where's yellow fish?
Where's yellow fish?

Poor yellow fish lost its way.

How many feet?

How many feet?

Two little feet in the bay.

Where's the red pail?
Where's the red pail?

Two little feet dash away.

One happy fish.
One happy fish.

One happy fish on its way!

How many fish?
How many fish?

Six little fish in the bay!

About the Author and the Illustrator

Author

Caron Lee Cohen has always liked going to the beach. She likes to swim. She has seen many fish in the water!

Illustrator

S. D. Schindler was known for his drawings even as a child in school.

Mr. Schindler likes having fish around. He made two ponds near his house. They are filled with goldfish.

One, Two, Three, Four, Five
a Mother Goose rhyme

One, two, three, four, five,

Once I caught a fish alive,

Six, seven, eight, nine, ten,

Then I let it go again.

Why did you let it go?

Because it bit my finger so.

Which finger did it bite?

The little finger on the right.

Let's Talk

What would you do if you were the fish under the pail?

Fish in the Bay

What you need:

paper

crayons or markers

art supplies

What you do:

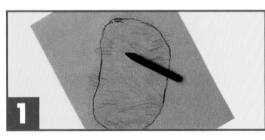

1

Draw some water.

Color it.

2

Draw some fish.

Cut them out.

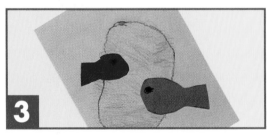

3

Paste the fish in the water.

4

Write the word that tells how many fish.

Funny Fish

The order of words tells
what a sentence means.
Which sentence tells
about the picture?

A fish is under a pail.
A pail is under a fish.

Talk

Look at the picture.
Which sentence tells
about the picture?

A crab feeds a fish.
A fish feeds a crab.

Write

Work with your class.
Write funny sentences
about fish.
Make a funny fish poem.

141

JOG, FROG, JOG

by Barbara Gregorich
illustrated by Bernard Adnet

This is a frog.

The frog likes to jog.

He jogs in the day.

He jogs in the night.

Oh, oh! This is a dog.

The dog does not like frogs.

The dog sees the frog!

Jog, frog, jog!

Jog in the water!

Jog in the fog!

Go, frog, go!
Jog into the log!

The log stops the dog.

Jog, frog! Jog around that dog!

Poor dog!

Tadpole to Frog

by Fay Robinson

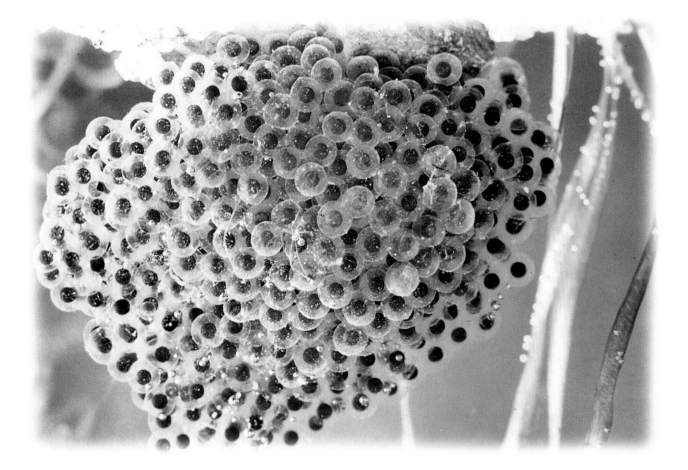

Here is some water.

Here are some eggs.

This is a tadpole.

Here come his legs!

His tail gets little.

His body gets plump.

Soon he's a frog.
Look at him jump!

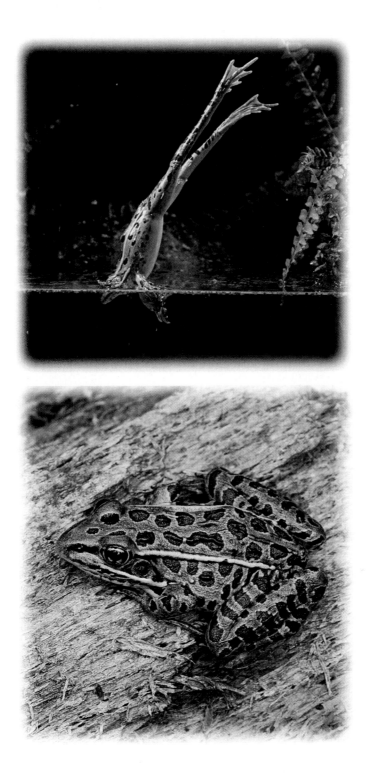

Where does he go?

Into water, on logs.

We like to see tadpoles
turn into frogs!

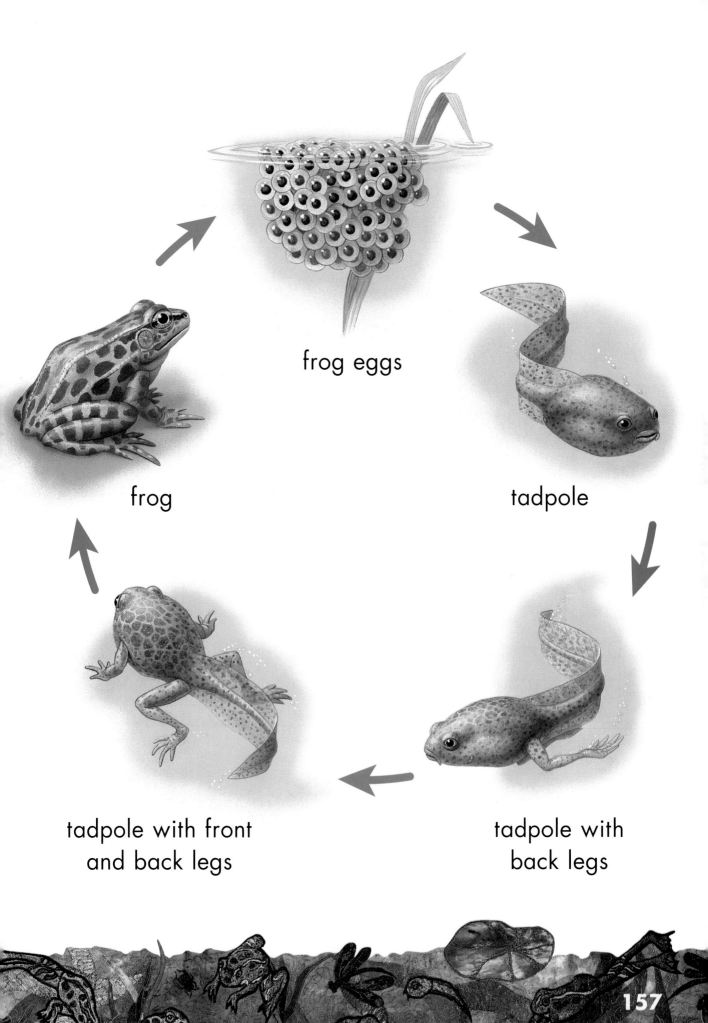

frog eggs

tadpole

frog

tadpole with front
and back legs

tadpole with
back legs

About the Author

Fay Robinson

Do you think spiders, snakes, beetles, lizards, and frogs are creepy? Fay Robinson doesn't. She loves writing about them. She thinks that they are fun to learn about.

Ms. Robinson was a teacher before she became a writer. She and her students raised tadpoles. Every morning her students would check to find out if the tadpoles had changed.

Notice

by David McCord

I have a dog,
I had a cat.
I've got a frog
Inside my hat.

Let's Talk

Were you surprised by the way the tadpole grew? Why or why not?

Make a Frog Book

What did you learn about tadpoles and frogs?

1. Write a fact about a tadpole or frog.
2. Then draw something about that fact.
3. Put your page in a class book.

At the Pond

A **telling sentence** tells something.

It begins with a capital letter.

It ends with a . .

The frog jumps.

This is a telling sentence.

It tells what a frog does.

Talk

Look at the picture.
Tell something about
the picture.
Use a telling sentence.

Write

Write a telling sentence
about a water animal.

A Big Job

by Kana Riley

illustrated by Stacey Schuett

The sun is hot.

Birds sing.

Mom is singing too.

She digs and digs.

She does not stop.

Beans go in the dirt.

Mom is watering the beans.

Look at them go.

They do not stop.

Mom gets a pot.

She picks the beans one
by one.

Mom is filling the
pot to the top.
It is a big job.

Mom is licking her lips.

I am too.

It is time to eat.

We eat the beans one
by one.

Sweet Potato Pie

by Anne Rockwell
illustrated by Carolyn Croll

Pa picks sweet potatoes
one by one.

Why, oh, why?

Sweet potato pie!

Grandma bakes them
till they're done.

Why, oh, why?
Sweet potato pie!

Gramps stops chopping.

Ma stops washing.

Tom stops swimming.
Why, oh, why?

Sis stops
swinging.

Bob starts singing.

Come and get my
sweet potato pie!

Everybody coming
one by one.

Why, oh, why?
Sweet potato pie!

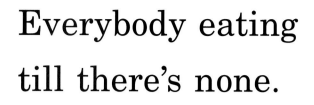

Everybody eating
till there's none.

My, oh, my.
Sweet potato pie!

About the Author

Anne Rockwell

As a child, Anne Rockwell often visited her grandparents. They lived on a farm in Mississippi. They grew their own food as the family in *Sweet Potato Pie* did.

Ms. Rockwell remembers her grandmother telling stories in the kitchen. Her grandmother read to her too. She taught Ms. Rockwell to love reading.

Let's Talk

The people in the story liked the smell of sweet potato pie. What food smells very good to you?

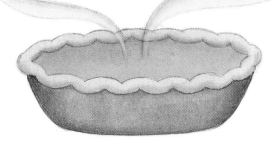

Act Out the Story

1. Read the story aloud with your classmates.
2. Take turns acting out each part.

What Do You Like?

A **question** asks something.

A question is an asking sentence.

It begins with a capital letter.

It ends with a **?** .

Who made the pizza**?**

This is a question.

It asks something.

Talk

Ask a question about the picture.

Have someone answer your question.

Write

Write a question about yourself.

Then write the answer.

Pictionary

Animals

Pets

cat

dog

Farm Animals

pig

hog

horse

cow

Bird

duck

Insect

ant

190

Wild Animals

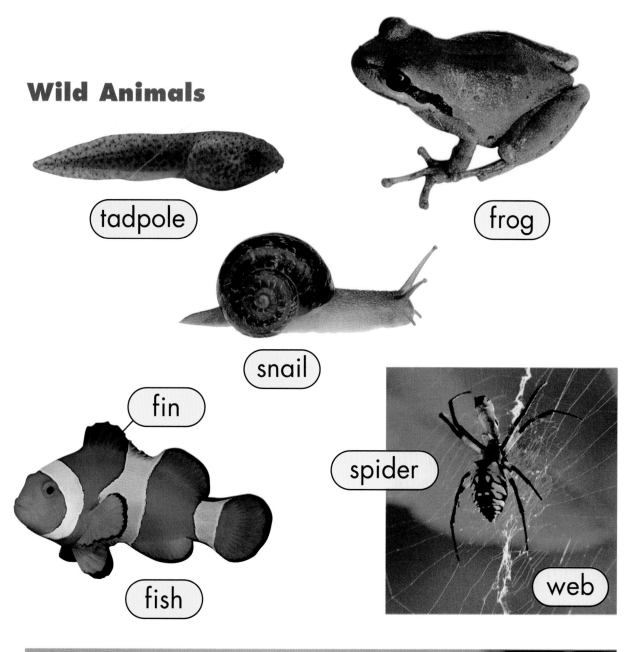

tadpole

frog

snail

fin

fish

spider

web

bear

cub

Tested Word List

The Nap
Oh, Cats!

away
come
down
no
will

What Did I See?
I Went Walking

did
me
saw
walk
went

Jog, Frog, Jog
Tadpole to Frog

does
he
into
this
water

Look at That!
Can You Find It?

all
are
find
make
play

Fish Mix
How Many Fish?

happy
how
many
on
they
why

A Big Job
Sweet Potato Pie

by
eat
sing
stop
them

Acknowledgments

Text
Page 18: *Oh, Cats!* by Nola Buck, pictures by Nadine Bernard Westcott, pp. 4–24. Text copyright © 1997 by Nola Buck. Illustrations copyright © 1997 by Nadine Bernard Westcott, Inc. Reprinted by permission of HarperCollins Publishers, Inc.
Page 76: *I Went Walking* by Sue Williams, illustrated by Julie Vivas. Text copyright © 1989 by Sue Williams. Illustrations copyright © 1989 by Julie Vivas. Reprinted by permission of Harcourt Brace & Company.
Page 107: "Quack, Quack!" from *Oh, Say Can You Say?* by Dr. Seuss. Copyright © 1979 by Dr. Seuss Enterprises, L.P. Reprinted by permission of Random House, Inc.
Page 118: *How Many Fish?* by Caron Lee Cohen, pictures by S. D. Schindler, pp. 6–25. Text copyright © 1998 by Caron Lee Cohen. Illustrations copyright © 1998 by S. D. Schindler. Reprinted by permission of HarperCollins Publishers, Inc.
Page 142: *Jog, Frog, Jog* by Barbara Gregorich, pp. 2, 4, 6, 8, 10, 12, 14, 16, 18, 20, 22, 24, 26, 28, & 30. Copyright © 1992 by School Zone ® Publishing Company. Reprinted by permission of School Zone ® Publishing Company.
Page 159: "Notice" from *One at a Time* by David McCord. Copyright 1952 by David McCord. Reprinted by permission of Little, Brown and Company.
Page 170: *Sweet Potato Pie* by Anne Rockwell, pp. 5, 7–9, 11, 13, 15, 17–18, 20, 23, 25, 27–28, 30, & 32. Text copyright © 1996 by Anne Rockwell. Reprinted by permission of Random House, Inc.

Artists
Maryjane Begin, cover, 8–9
Jackie Urbanovic, 10–17
Nadine Bernard Westcott, 18–39
Clive Scruton, 40–41
Seth Larson, 42–49
Wendy Edelson, 50–65
George Ulrich, 66–67
Benton Mahan, 68–75
Julie Vivas, 76–106
Eileen Mueller-Neill, 107
Laura Ovresat, 108–109
S. D. Schindler, 118–137
Kathy Lengyel, 139
Susan Nethery, 141
Bernard Adnet, 142–149
Ellen Eddy, (border) 150
Walter Stuart, 157
Kathy McCord, 159
Pamela Paulsrud, (calligraphy) 159
Andrea Z. Tachiera, 160–161
Stacey Schuett, 162–169
Carolyn Croll, 170–189

Photographs
Page 39 (T) Courtesy HarperCollins Publishers
Page 106 (TL) Courtesy Harcourt Brace & Company, Photo: Doug Nicholas; (TR) Courtesy Harcourt Brace & Company
Pages 110, 111, 112 (TL, BCL, BCR, BL, BR) Norbert Wu
Page 112 (TR) Steven David Miller/Animals Animals/Earth Scenes; (TCL) Andrew G. Wood/Photo Researchers; (TCR) Carl Roessler/Tony Stone Images
Page 113 (TL, TR) Norbert Wu; (TCL, TCR) Superstock, Inc.; (BCL) Fred Bavendam/Minden Pictures; (BCR) M. Gibbs/OSF/Animals Animals/Earth Scenes; (BL, BR) Norbert Wu
Page 114 M. Gibbs/OSF/Animals Animals/Earth Scenes
Page 115 James D. Watt/Mo Yung Productions/Norbert Wu
Pages 116, 117 Norbert Wu
Page 138 (TL) Courtesy Caron Lee Cohen, Photo: Elaine B. Cohen; (C) Kip Simons for Scott Foresman
Page 150 Nathan Cohen/Visuals Unlimited
Page 151 Harry Rogers/NAS/Photo Researchers
Page 152 John Mitchell/Photo Researchers
Page 153 Harry Rogers/NAS/Photo Researchers
Pages 154, 155 (T) Stephen Dalton/Photo Researchers
Page 155 B Rod Planck/TOM STACK & ASSOCIATES
Page 156 Stephen Dalton/Photo Researchers
Page 158 (CR, CL, BR, TR) PhotoDisc, Inc.; (TC) Ron Davis for Scott Foresman
Page 187 Courtesy Anne Rockwell
Page 190 cat, dog, pig, horse, cow, duck, PhotoDisc, Inc.; ant, Artville
Page 191 tadpole, Harry Rogers/NAS/Photo Researchers; frog, spider/web, bear/cub, PhotoDisc, Inc.; snail, Artville